P9-DCI-516

LET'S-READ-AND-FIND-OUT SCIENCE®

POP!
A Book About
BUBBLES

STAGE 1

by Kimberly Brubaker Bradley

photographs by Margaret Miller

HarperCollins*Publishers*

Guilderland Public Library
2228 Western Avenue
Guilderland, NY 12084-9701

To Meemaw, Queen of Bubbles,
and to Matthew and Katie, Chief Bubble Blowers
—K.B.B.

I want to thank the children in this book who blew bubbles with
grace and gusto: Emily Brigstocke, Pearson and Katherine Miller,
Christopher and Chloe Nelson, Durango Petit,
Ashley Sherman, and Jillian Williams.
—M.M.

The *Let's-Read-and-Find-Out Science* book series was originated by Dr. Franklyn M. Branley, Astronomer Emeritus and former Chairman of the American Museum—Hayden Planetarium, and was formerly co-edited by him and Dr. Roma Gans, Professor Emeritus of Childhood Education, Teachers College, Columbia University. Text and illustrations for each of the books in the series are checked for accuracy by an expert in the relevant field. For more information about Let's-Read-and-Find-Out Science books, write to HarperCollins Children's Books, 1350 Avenue of the Americas, New York, NY 10019, or visit our website at www.letsreadandfindout.com.

HarperCollins®, 🅿®, and Let's Read-and-Find-Out Science® are trademarks of HarperCollins Publishers Inc.

POP! *A Book About Bubbles*
Text copyright © 2001 by Kimberly Brubaker Bradley
Illustrations copyright © 2001 by Margaret Miller
Printed in the U.S.A. All rights reserved.

Library of Congress Cataloging-in-Publication Data
Bradley, Kimberly Brubaker.
    Pop! : a book about bubbles / by Kimberly Brubaker Bradley; photographs by Margaret Miller.
        p.   cm. — (Let's-read-and-find-out science. Stage 1)
    Summary: Simple text explains how soap bubbles are made, why they are always round, and why they pop.
    ISBN 0-06-028700-4 — ISBN 0-06-028701-2 (lib. bdg.) — ISBN 0-06-445208-5 (pbk.)
    1. Soap bubbles—Juvenile literature.   [1. Soap bubbles.   2. Bubbles.]   I. Miller, Margaret, 1945– ill.   II. Title.   III. Series.
QC183.B795   2001   99-57794
530.4'275—dc21

Typography by Elynn Cohen ❖ 1   2   3   4   5   6   7   8   9   10 First Edition

POP!
A Book About
BUBBLES

Dip the plastic wand into the soap solution.

Hold it up to your mouth.

Now blow.

Phhhh! You've made a bubble!

Watch it float higher and higher.
The bubble shimmers in the sun.
Up it goes, up, up, then *pop!*
It disappears.

You can blow small bubbles or big ones.

You can blow one bubble or hundreds of bubbles.

You can't blow square bubbles or flat bubbles.

All bubbles are round.

Bubbles are air trapped inside liquid.

The liquid you put your bubble wand into is made of water and soap. Sometimes it has a little corn syrup too.

It is sticky. It sticks to the floor if you spill it. It sticks to your fingers when you touch it. And it sticks to the plastic bubble wand. It sticks and it stretches. It stretches across the round hole on the end of the bubble wand.

When you blow into the wand,
you make air move.

If you blow slowly, you can
see how the air makes the
soap on the wand start to

s t r e t c h .

As you blow harder, the soap stretches and stretches until it can't stretch anymore. Finally it snaps free. The soap shuts around the air inside it. There it is! A bubble!

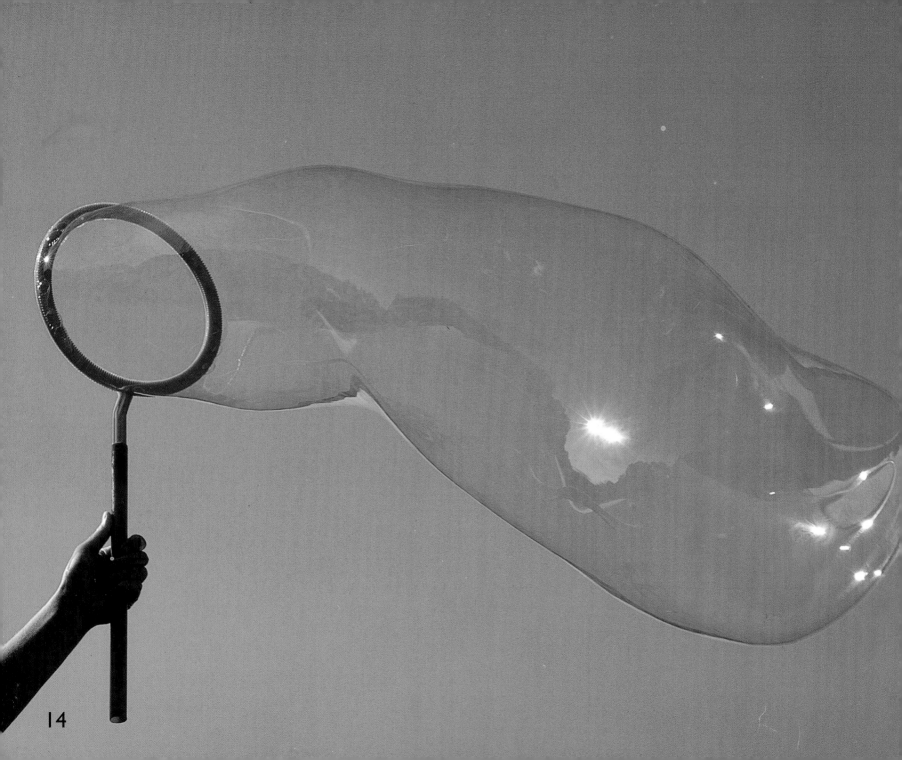

14

You don't have to blow to make a bubble. If you hold your bubble wand up to the wind, the wind will blow bubbles for you. You can also make bubbles by holding the wand up and running. Anything that moves air can make a bubble.

If a bubble touches something, like your hand or another bubble, it may have a flat side. Or the wind may push a bubble and change its shape.

But when a bubble is quietly floating in the air by itself, it is always round.

The air inside the bubble pushes out against the soap skin. It doesn't push harder in one place than in another. It pushes evenly in every direction. This makes the bubble round.

The soap skin holds the air inside. It pushes back against the air.

If your hands are dry and you touch bubbles, they pop. Anything that pokes them makes a hole in the soap skin. *Whoosh!* The air inside rushes out.

Even if you don't touch bubbles, they still pop. They dry out. Their soap skins shrink. Soon they can't hold all the air inside them. *Pop!*

There are other kinds of bubbles, too. The next time you drink soda, look carefully at the bottom of the glass. You will see tiny bubbles forming. You can watch them get **bigger** and **bigger**.

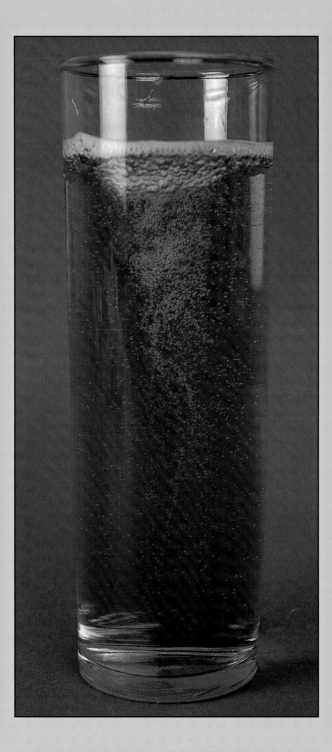

Finally they get so big that they start to float up through the soda—higher and higher, then *pop!*

You can also make bubbles with a straw. Put one end of the straw in a glass of water or juice and blow. Bubbles float up through the liquid and pop. Water and juice aren't sticky like soap solution, so the bubbles pop right away.

Milk is stickier than water. If you blow bubbles with a straw in a glass of milk, they will stay at the top of the glass for a while. They won't float through the air like soap bubbles. The milk isn't sticky enough for that. But milk bubbles look like soap bubbles. Wherever they aren't touching the glass or each other, they will be round.

You can make tiny, tiny bubbles.

You can make bubbles big enough to step inside.

You can blow one bubble or a whole stream of bubbles.

But you can't make square bubbles.
Bubbles are always round.

An Easy Way to Make Bubble Solution

You will need:

- a measuring spoon (any size; use a cup if you want to make a LOT of bubbles)
- liquid dishwashing soap (for washing dishes by hand, not for automatic dishwashers)
- a bowl
- corn syrup
- water

1. Pour one spoonful of liquid dishwashing soap into the bowl.

2. Pour one spoonful of corn syrup into the bowl.

3. Pour nine spoonfuls of water into the bowl. Stir very gently, so you don't make foam.

4. Find a wand and blow some bubbles! You can use a wand that came with bubble solution you bought at the store. Or you can make a wand out of wire. You can even blow bubbles with your fingers. Make a circle with your thumb and fingers, dip it in the bubble solution, and blow!

Note: This bubble solution uses ingredients you probably already have in your cupboard. You can make bubbles that last a little longer if you use a spoonful of glycerin instead of corn syrup. You can find glycerin in some drugstores. All bubbles solutions are sticky. Blow bubbles outside, so you don't make a mess in your house.

Bubble Experiments

Are bubbles always round?

The hole on most bubble wands is round. If you blew bubbles through a square hole, would they be square bubbles? Find out!

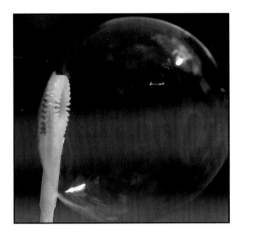

Take a quart- or pint-size milk carton and have a grown-up carefully cut off both ends. Dip one end into the bubble solution and blow a bubble. What shape is it?

You can also use wire to make bubble wands in lots of different shapes. You can make wands with holes that are rectangular, triangular, or square. What shapes will the bubbles be?

How slow can you blow?

When you blow into a bubble wand, you are moving air. When you blow softly, you move air slowly. When you blow hard, you move air fast.

Blow into a bubble wand as softly as you can. How many bubbles did you make? How big were they?

Now blow as hard as you can. (Hint: Blow steadily, as if you are blowing out the candles on a birthday cake. Don't blow in one big puff!) How many bubbles did you make? How big were they?

Can you figure out what is happening? When you blow slowly, you stretch the bubble solution slowly. When you blow fast, you stretch the solution fast. How does this change the size of the bubbles? How does it change how many bubbles you get?